I0011697

Learn Web Design with HTML examples and screen shots

Ohwofosirai Desmond

DEDICATION

This book is dedicated to those who love HTML programming. Most especially those who do not like the use of lazy man tools like frontpage, dreamweaver, amongst others. I am dedicated to help you grow your knowledge and programming skill as much as you would love. Thanks.

CONTENT

ACKNOWLEDGEMENT

I would like to acknowledge the person of Tamada Srinivas- the man that brought me this vision of blogging and teaching web design on the internet I would also appreciate Mr. Ohwofosirai Einstein for all the time we share together.

1 HTML INTRODUCTION

HTML means Hyper Text Markup Language. Generally, HTML is not considered a programming language, but a markup language. HTML uses what we call "markup tags" to describe how a web page would look.

A web browser interprets markup tags i.e. it reads through the HTML documents and displays them as web pages. The general format for all HTML documents is given below.

Consider the general format:

```
<html>
<head>
<title>My first example crying out loud</title>
</head>
<body>
<h1> Some big heading</h1>
<p> paragraph example</p>
</body>
</html>
```

Explanation

The contents in between <html> and </html> determine the entire web page layout and display. The texts between <body> and </body> would be the only visible items on page. The heading text appear between <h1> and </h1>. The text between <p> and </p> is displayed on a new paragraph

You should copy the code in the box above to notepad. Save it on desktop. To save it, type "my_example_1.htm" as your chosen file name. Make sure you select files of type "all file" before saving. If it's correctly saved, the icon which shows on the desktop is that of your default browser i.e. Mozilla or Opera. Now, Click on it to see how it is on the browser. Hmm, oh! Cheers! Congrats! You are now a programmer. This is your first working code.

As we proceed, just copy the codes and try them out.

2 HTML- STARTING REQUIREMENT

Software Requirements:
You need no special software to do HTML programing. You don't need an HTML editor or even a web server. Notepad is ok.
In this tutorial, i would use Notepad. I think it's the best for a beginer.
However, a professional web developer would prefer HTML editors like FrontPage or Dreamweaver, instead of using notepad.

File Extension Requirement:
You can save an HTML file with either the ".htm" or the ".html" extension. If you don't do this, your work would not be recognised as an html document.

3 HTML FORMATTING EXAMPLES

HTML Headings

For HTML headings we use the <h1> to <h6> tags. <h1> defines the largest heading. <h6> defines the smallest heading.
Example
<h1>Largest heading</h1>
<h2>2nd level heading</h2>
<h3>Smallest heading</h3>

The codes above when viewed on a web browser would display like this:
Largest heading

2nd level heading

Smallest heading

Note:
Web browsers would normally add an empty line before and after each heading. Please, don't use headings instead of <strong>.
Headings are not meant to be used in the place of tags that ensure bold text.
It is important for ease of access if you structure your page properly by using appropriate headings in your document.
H1 headings should be used as main headings. You must not include more than one H1 per webpage. This is generally a search engine optimization rule.

HTML Links

HTML links are defined with the <a> tag.
Example
<a href=http://23cliques.com rel="nofollow">This is a link</a>

When search engines encounter a *'rel="follow"'*, it will craw the link. If it encounters *'rel="nofollow"'*, the search engine will not craw that link. So pages

from that link would not be indexed. You may use it if the link on your site points to another site whose content are not related to yours.
Note: The link address is provided as an attribute.

HTML Elements

An HTML element has a start tag and an end tag. Some HTML elements have no text between the start and end tags. They are empty. Empty elements are normally closed within the start tag e.g <br/>. Most HTML elements can have attributes e.g <form name="registration_form">

Note: HTML elements may be nested (an HTML element can be found within another HTML element).

See nexted Document Example
<html>
<body>
<p>This paragraph nexted within body tag and body tag within html tag</p>
</body>
</html>

Other Information:

Case sensitivity:

HTML tags are not case sensitive: <i> is the same as <I>.

Include end tag always

Most browsers will display HTML document correctly even if you forget the end tag:
<p>wrong paragraph style
<p>second wrong paragraph

The example above will work in many web browsers, but don't do it. Omitting the end tag can make formatting the page layout difficult for you.

HTML Comments

Comments can be inserted in the HTML code to make it more readable and understandable. Comments are ignored by the browser and are not displayed. Comments are written like this:

Example

<!-- This is a comment -->

Note: There is an exclamation point after the opening bracket, but not before the closing bracket

4 HTML ATTRIBUTES

Attributes provide more or extra information about HTML elements. For example size (of textbox), name (of field), etc.

Attributes gives extra information about an element. It should be specified in the start tag always. Attributes always occur as name/value pairs like this: *attribute name="its value"*. In form it looks like this example: *<input type="file"/>*

The "type" which comes after "input" is an attribute of the input element.

Attribute example here:
HTML links are defined with the <a> tag. The link address is provided as an attribute of element a.
Example
<a href="http://www.23cliques.com">This is a link</a>

"href" is the attribute of <a> tag: Its value equal the link address. Within the <a> tag, you can add other attributes like "rel" and "title".

Do always enclose all attribute values within quotes. You can use double or single style quote. In some situations when the attribute value itself contains quotes, it is necessary to use single quotes:
* *

5 HTML PROGRAMMING EXAMPLES

Horizontal Rule

You can create an horizontal line in the web browser by using this simple code:
Example below:
<hr/>
The line would show in your browser like the one below
_____

HTML Line Breaks

Use the <br /> tag if you want a line break (a new line) without starting a new paragraph:
Example
<p>This is
a para
graph with line breaks</p>

The <br /> element is an empty HTML element. It has no end tag.
This is how the code in the box would show in a web browser:
This is
A para
Graph with line breaks

Html Text Formating

This text is really bold
This text is italic! Wow!
This is normal computer output
This is $_{subscript}$ and ^{superscript}
HTML uses tags like <b> and <i> for making texts bold and *italic*.
Examples:
My name is <b> Desmond</b>
You are <i>talking</i> too much

Would look like this:
My name is Desmond.
You are *talking* too much

Tags like the ones used above are called formatting tags.

Preformatted Text

Any text that comes within the <pre> tag is preformatted. As a result, it does not take the properties of its parent. For example,

<p style="color:red; width:50px">
<pre>Joke</pre>
</p>

The word "joke" is within a paragraph "<p>", any text within this paragraph is supposed to be at most 50px and red in color. But "Joke" will never take such properties because its within a <pre> tag.

Quotations

Quotations are either long or short. See the example below:

<blockquote>
Tough times never last, but tough people do
........Clement Rubber Stamp
</blockquote>

Delete and insert text.

You've probably noticed a line strike through texts like this:

~~$45~~

Formally, the <strike> tag is used. But, it's deprecated.

Modern browsers support <del> tag.

Using the <del> tag, you strike through a text as follows:

<del>$45</del>

You insert text using:

<ins>Just enter your text here...</ins>

The output looks just like:

Just enter your text here...

6 HTML STYLES

The introduction of inline style enabled us do better design- with CSS codes introduced into HTML. Observe the difference in texts shown below:

Look! Styles and colors
This text is in Verdana
This text is in Arial
This text is 30 pixels high

The Inline-Style

The purpose of the style attribute is to give a web page a beautiful look and feel.

With Inline-styles, properties or attributes are assigned to an element directly without using a separate style sheets (CSS files).

You can learn more about styles and CSS in our CSS Programming Guide.

HTML Inline Style Examples

style="background-color:yellow"
style="font-size:10px"
style="font-family:Tahoma"
style="text-align:center"

Some tags are no more recommended for use: so avoid them. In the examples below, you will see a better way of doing things:

Background Color

<body style="background-color:#ffffff"></body>
The style attribute above defines a style for the <body> element.
The code above would display the background color below:

#ffffff is color code for white. That explains the reason for the white space above. You can try by replacing white with other color names you know.
The new style attribute makes the "old" bgcolor attribute obsolete.

Background the old way

```
<table border="1" bgcolor="black">
<tr><td>
 
</td></tr>
</table>
```

Font Family, Color and Size

```
<p style="font-family:courier new; background-color:white; color:black; font-size:20px">
Hi Steve!
</p>
```
Preview here:
Hi Steve!
The new style attribute makes the old <font> tag obsolete.

Fonts the old way

```
<font size="12px" color="black">
Hi Steve!
</font>
```

Text Alignment

The style attribute defines a style for the <h1> element.
```
<h1 style="text-align:center">
Blood Groups
</h1>
```
The output in a web browser:

Blood Groups

The new style attribute makes the old "align" attribute obsolete.

Centered heading the old way

```
<center>
<h1>Blood Groups<h1>
</center>
```

7 HTML IMAGE

HTML images are defined with the <img> tag.
You insert an image to your web page by using the code below:
Example:
<img src="mountain.jpg" width="104" height="142" alt="Trip to Norwey" />

Note:
For the example above, you have to place the image file "mountain.jpg" in the same folder with your web project file. Else, you can use a url.
The name and the size of the image are provided as attributes.
You noticed the introduction of four attributes- src, width, height and alt.
Width and height help you resize the image shown.

Example

Insert images from different locations

These examples demonstrate how to insert an image from another folder or another server. You can only access files via relative path when you have a web server installed.

Relative Path

If you have a folder named "www" which contain your web files, and your images saved to another folder named "images" such that images is inside www folder, your images can be accessed as "images/name_of_image". For example,
<img src="images/dexmundo.jpg" alt="author">
If you have a folder named "www" which contain your web files, and your images saved to another folder named "images" such that images is outside

12

www, your images can be accessed as "/images/name_of_image". For example,

<img src="/images/dexmundo.jpg" alt="developer">

If the image file and the file containing your html code are on the same folder, you simply access the file by specifying its name.

<img src="dexmundo.jpg" alt="Microblinks CEO">

Absolute Path

If the image is located somewhere on the internet, you enter the full path beginning with http://.

That will look like this: *<img src="http://www.23cliques.com/dexmundo.jpg">*

You can also access files on your hard drive by specifying the absolute path. For example,

<img src="C:\wamp\www\image\dexmundo.jpg">

Image Tag and Src Attribute

In HTML, images are defined with the <img> tag.

To display an image on a web page, you need to use the src attribute. Src points to file source. The value of the src attribute is the path to the image you want to display on your page.

So the syntax is like this:

<img src="url" />

URL in example above refers to the location where the image is stored. An image named "mygoat.gif" located in the directory "images" on "www.23cliques.com" has the URL: http://www.23cliques.com/images/mygoat.gif.

The Alt Attribute

The alt attribute is used to assign an "alternate text" for an image. An alternate text shows if image is missing or maybe did not load properly. The value of the alt attribute is as defined by the developer:

<img src="mygoat.gif" alt="my goat" />

It is very good to always include the "alt" attribute an image. "Alt" is very important to search engines too.

Precaution: Use Image Carefully

Loading images take time so use image carefully. Also not all image formats are compatible with the html. Use jpeg, png, tiff and gif images.

Background image

This is how you add a background image to an HTML page:

```
<p style="background-image:url(dexmundo.png);">
 <! -Enter Texts here-->
</p>
```

Instead of a background color, the image named "dexmundo.jpg" becomes the background image. You can replace dexmundo.jpg with either a relative or absolute path or even a url. It depends on the location of the image file you want to access. When accessing an image on the internet, you must begin with http://.

Aligning images

Text around an image can be aligned at the top, bottom, middle and base. You only change the vertical align property to any of these four. See our example below:

```
<p>
<img src="" style="width:100px; height:90px;vertical-align:middle"/>
Hi reader, I am Ohwofosirai Desmond, CEO of Emmablinks.
</p
```

Let The Image Float

A text or image can either float to the right or left of a page. By default, it floats left. In this example, we will demonstrate how an image can float to the left or right of a paragraph.

```
<p style="border: 1px solid #aaaaaa">
<img src="dexmundo.jpg" style="float:left"/>
</p>
```

See it in the figure below:

14

As you see, the image on the screen left. You can make it float right instead of the normal left direction. You can alter that by changing float direction to right.

Hyperlink an image

You can turn an image to a hyperlink, so that when a user clicks it, it opens a new web address. Find the code below:

```
<a href="http://23cliques.com/index.php">
<img src="23CliqueLogo.png" alt="Visit 23"/>
</a>
```

You can replace http://23cliques.com/index.php with any website url of your choice.

8 HTML TABLES

Sometimes the lines within a table are visible, but it is not always visible. An HTML table looks like this:

HTML Tables

Rice	500kg
Okra|	45kg

Tables begin with <table> tag. A table is divided into rows- using <tr> tag and each row consists of cells- created using <td> tag.

<table border="1">
<tr>
<td>1st row, 1st cell </td>
<td>1st row, 2nd cell </td>
</tr>
<tr>
<td>2nd row, 1st cell </td>
<td>2nd row, 2nd cell </td>
</tr>
</table>

How it looks in a browser:

1st row, 1st cell	1st row, 2nd cell
2nd row, 1st cell	2nd row, 2nd cell

Table Border

If you do not specify a border attribute the table will have no borders- so if you want to see the border, do specify. To display a table with borders, you will have to use the border attribute- assign it a value of 1 (show border) or 0 (don't show border).

Table Headings

We define table headings using <th> tag.

```
<table border="1">
<tr>
<th>Ist Column Heading</th>
<th>2nd Column Heading</th>
</tr>
<tr>
<td>1,1</td>
<td>1,2</td>
</tr>
<tr>
<td>2,1</td>
<td>2,2</td>
</tr>
</table>
```

How it looks in a browser:

Ist Column Heading	2nd Column Heading
1,1	1,2
2,1	2,2

Now, you can change *border="1"* to *border="0"* and see how it look.

Table With Empty Cells

Empty table cells do not display correctly in some browsers. You would see this in the examples we will give you.

```
<table border="1">
<tr>
<td>1, 1</td>
<td>1, 2</td>
</tr>
<tr>
<td>2, 1</td>
<td></td>
</tr>
</table>
```

17

How it looks in a browser:

1,1	1,2
2,1	

Note: borders around the empty cell don't show except in Mozilla Firefox.
To avoid this error, add a non-breaking space ( ) to empty cells. That will make the borders visible in all browsers:

```
<table border="1">
<tr>
<td>row 1, cell 1</td>
<td>row 1, cell 2</td>
</tr>
<tr>
<td>row 2, cell 1</td>
<td> </td>
</tr>
</table>
```

How it looks in a browser:

row 1, cell 1	row 1, cell 2
row 2, cell 1	

Like I said before, the borders you see around the table above would be invisible if you change the border attribute inside table tag to zero (0) instead of one (1). Example as follows:

```
<table border="0">
........
</table>
```

Table cells that span more than one row/column

You must have seen a table like this before.

Did you ever wonder how to do it in HTML? Well, it's possible. You only need two more attributes called "rowspan" and "colspan"- depending on whether you merge row or columns.

The code below explains how to define table cells that span more than one row or one column.

```
<table width="300px" border="1">
<tr><td colspan="2"> </td></tr>
<tr><td> </td><td> </td></tr>
<tr><td rowspan="2"> </td><td> </td></tr>
<tr><td> </td></tr>
</table>
```

Explanation: There are four rows, two columns in the above table. In our code, each row begins with a <tr> tag. <td> tag creates a cell within a new row. Colspan='2' mean this cell takes two columns- this one and the immediate next. So no needs for another <td> tag to create a second cell. Rowspan='2' mean this cell takes this row and the one under it. So no need for two <td> tags in the following row because one is taken already.

Cellpadding and cellspacing

Cellpadding refer to the white space between the cell content and its borders while cellspacing is the distance between the cells. Now see what will happen to the thickness of your table border if you try out this code:

```
<table width="300px" border="1" cellpadding="3" cellspacing="0">
<tr><td>laughing is sweet</td></tr>
</table>
```

The output should look like this:

Laughing is sweet

You will notice the line is thinner (cellspacing="0"). Also the text is far a little from the border (cellspacing="3"). You can try out other examples yourself.

Add a background color or a background image to a table
The best way to add a background color or background image is to introduce in-line CSS. For a background image or color, add the following to your <table> or <td> tag.
Background Color- Add *style="background-color:color code or color name"*
Background Image- Add *style="background-image:url(File Path)"*

For example, to create a table with black background and white text we do the following:
<table width="300px" border="1" style="background-color:black;color:white">
<tr><td align="center">laughing is good for you</td></tr>
</table>
We would have a table that looks like this:

Laughing is good for you

Align the content in a table cell.
You can align a table either to the left, right or center of the page. How? Just add:

<table align="right">
...Other contents here...
</table>

But if you like to change the alignment for texts in just one or more cells, then add "align='*the direction*'" within the cell's <td> tag. For example,
<table width="300px" border="1" cellpadding="3" cellspacing="0"
align="right">
<tr><td align="center">laughing is good for you</td></tr>
</table>

The table is moved away to the right side of the screen. Besides, out text "laughing is good for you" is now shown at the center of the table. You can also align texts using "justify".

9 HTML LISTS

HTML supports ordered, unordered and definition lists. An unordered list generally takes this form:

HTML Lists

I am unordered- but am sorry, it's not my fault.

That's why am like this. Other symbols can be used too.

If not I would have been numbered numerically, alphabetically or roman numerals.

Unordered Lists

Unordered list items are marked with small black circles i.e. bullets.

An unordered list starts with the <ul> tag. Each list item starts with the <li> tag.

```
<ul>
<li> Cowbell is sweet. It's our milk </li>
<li>Blue boat Milk is good for me</li>
</ul>
```

Here is how it looks in a browser:

- Cowbell is sweet. It's our milk
- Blue boat Milk is good for me

Inside a list item you can put paragraphs, line breaks, images, links, other lists, etc.

Ordered Lists

Ordered list items are marked either by alphabets, roman numerals or numbers.

An ordered list is defined with <ol> tag. Each list item starts with the <li> tag.

```
<ol>
<li>I love my mummy</li>
<li>Come and learn</li>
</ol>
```

Here is how it looks in a browser:

1. I love my mummy
2. Come and learn

Definition Lists

A definition list is not a list of single items- It is a list of items (or terms), with a description of each item (or term). A definition list starts with a <dl> tag (definition list). Each term starts with a <dt> tag (definition term). Each description starts with a <dd> tag (definition description).

```
<dl>
<dt>School</dt>
<dd>Aunty Maria Sec. School</dd>
<dt>Church</dt>
<dd>The Redeemed Family</dd>
</dl>
```
Here is how it looks in a browser:
School
     Aunty Maria Sec. School
Church
     The Redeemed Family
Inside the <dd> tag you can put paragraphs, line breaks, images, links, other lists, etc.

Ordered Lists: Different Types

By default, the ordered list has its content defined in a numeric order. You can change this by adding an attribute called type to <ol> tag. The new tag now looks like this:
```
<ol type="a">
...Some other codes...
</ol>
```

Whether you choose to have it in alphabetic or roman figures is all your choice Attribute "type" can have any of these values- a, A, i, or I. So change it to get what you want. To have it in numerals, don't add attribute called "type" to <ol> tag. Look at this code: It will order the list by using uppercase alphabets.
```
<h4>States In Nigeria:</h4>
<ol type="A">
 <li>Delta</li>
 <li>Benin</li>
 <li>Lagos</li>
```

```
</ol>
```
Now see how your code looks in a web browser:

States In Nigeria:

A.   Delta
B.   Benin
C.   Lagos

So, try out the roman numeral example yourself!

Unordered Lists: Different Types

The unordered list takes different form. You can see the various form as outlined in the examples below:

1.   Disc bullets.
2.   Circle bullets.
3.   Square bullets.

The codes below would produce the types of unordered lists you see above. I advice you try out these codes.

```
<h4>Disc bullets:</h4>
<ul style="list-style-type:disc">
 <li>James</li>
 <li>John</li>
 <li>Steve</li>
</ul>

<h4>Circle bullets:</h4>
<ul style="list-style-type:circle">
 <li>Church</li>
 <li>Mosque</li>
 <li>Temple</li>
</ul>

<h4>Square bullets:</h4>
<ul style="list-style-type:square">
 <li>Great</li>
 <li>Small</li>
 <li>Medium</li>
</ul>
```

Nested list

Lists can be nested i.e. such that an item is listed under another. Just take a look at the examples below:

```
<h4>Example on Nested List:</h4>
<ul>
 <li>Father</li>
 <li>Mother</li>
 <li>Children
 <ul>
  <li>Son</li>
  <li>Daughter</li>
  </ul>
 </li>
</ul>
```

In a web browser, your code would look like this:

A nested List:

.   Father
.   Mother
.   Children
      .   Son
      .   Daughter

Note: Inside a list item you can put paragraphs, line breaks, images, links, other lists, etc.

10 HTML FORMS AND INPUT

Forms

A form contains form elements. Form elements are things that allow the user to enter information. Example of form elements are: text fields, textarea fields, drop-down menus, radio buttons and checkboxes.
A form is defined using the <form> tag.
<form>
...input elements...
</form>

Input

The most used form tag is the <input> tag. The type of input is specified with the type attribute. The most commonly used input types are explained below.

Text Fields

Text fields are used when you want the user to type letters, numbers, etc. in a form.
<form>
First name:
<input type="text" name="firstname" />
*
*
Last name:
<input type="text" name="lastname" />
</form>
How it looks in a browser:

First name:

Last name:

Note that the form itself is not visible. Also note that in most browsers, the width of the text field is 20 characters by default.

Radio Buttons

Radio Buttons are used when you want the user to select one of a limited number of choices.

```
<form>
<input type="radio" name="sex" value="male" /> Male
<br />
<input type="radio" name="sex" value="female" /> Female
</form>
```

How it looks in a browser:

☐ Male

☐ Female

Note that only one option can be chosen.

Checkboxes

Checkboxes are used when you want the user to select one or more options of a limited number of choices.

```
<form>
I have a bike:
<input type="checkbox" name="vehicle" value="Bike" />
<br />
I have a car:
<input type="checkbox" name="vehicle" value="Car" />
<br />
I have an airplane:
<input type="checkbox" name="vehicle" value="Airplane" />
</form>
```

How it looks in a browser:

I have a bike: ☐

I have a car: ☐

I have an airplane: ☐

Textarea

A text-area is a multi-line text input control. A user can write text in the text-area. In a text-area you can write an unlimited number of characters.

```
<textarea rows="10" cols="30"> The cat was playing in the garden. </textarea>
```

Your browser sees this code like this:

The cat was playing in the garden.

Fieldset around data

This example demonstrates how to draw a border with a caption around your data.

```
<form action="">
<fieldset>
<legend>Personal information:</legend>
Name: <input type="text" size="30"><br>
E-mail: <input type="text" size="30"><br>
Date of birth: <input type="text" size="10">
</fieldset>
</form>
```

Please feel your code in a web browser.

```
┌─ Personal information: ──────────────────────────────┐
│                                                       │
│  Name: [                              ]               │
│                                                       │
│  E-mail: [                            ]               │
│                                                       │
│  Date of birth: [          ]                          │
│                                                       │
└───────────────────────────────────────────────────────┘
```

Simple Drop-Down Box

The code below is used to create a simple drop-down box.

```
<form action="">
<select name="cars">
<option value="volvo">Volvo</option>
<option value="saab">Saab</option>
<option value="fiat">Fiat</option>
```

```
<option value="audi">Audi</option>
</select>
</form>
```

Your code should look like this:

The first content of the first <option> tag is chosen as the default value. However, you can alter it by making another option default. You only add attribute "selected" to the <option> tag whose content you prefer to make default. You simply add *"selected=selected"* to one of the option tags to make its content default. It would look like this:
<option value="audi" selected="selected">Audi</option>

Create a button
You can also create a button using <button> tag. It allows you define your text. However, button may require you know something about JavaScript. Buttons return control to JavaScript most times after an event is triggered. The code is given below:
<button type="button">Search this site</button>

Ensure you try out this code on your own.

The Form's Action & Submit Button
When the user clicks on the "Submit" button, the content of the form is sent to the server. The form's action attribute defines the name of the file to send the content to. The file defined in the action attribute usually does something with the received input.
<form name="input" action="form_submit.php" method="get">
Username:

```
<input type="text" name="user" />
<input type="submit" value="Submit" />
</form>
```

How it looks in a browser:

Username: [   ] Submit

If you type some characters in the text field, and click the "Submit" button, the browser will send your form data to a script file named "form_submit.php" for processing. But currently, that will do nothing because you don't have any PHP script named "form_submit.php".

You must learn a scripting language (e.g PHP) to be able to handle form submission and database operations.

To learn more about PHP form processing, read our PHP Programmer Guide.

11 HTML FRAMES

With frames, you can display the contents of more than one HTML document in the same browser window. Each unique webpage or document is called a frame, and each frame is independent of the others.

Frames have many disadvantages. First, the web developer must keep track of all the HTML documents used. Secondly, it is difficult to print the entire page. Lastly, frames are not search engine friendly- so avoid them.

The Frameset Tag

The <frameset> tag divides the window into frames. Each frameset defines a set of rows or columns. The values of the rows/columns determine the amount of space each row/column will take.

The Frame Tag

In the example below we have a frameset with two columns. The first column is set to 40% of the width of the browser window. The second column is set to 60% of the width of the browser window. The HTML document "frame_a.htm" is put into the first column, and the HTML document "frame_b.htm" is put into the second column:

<frameset cols="40%,60%">
  <frame src="frame_a.htm">
  <frame src="frame_b.htm">
</frameset>

Note:
The frameset column size value can also be set in pixels (cols="250,450") and one of the columns can be set to use the remaining space (cols="25%,*").

If a frame has visible borders, the user can resize it by dragging the border. To prevent a user from doing this, you can add noresize="noresize" to the <frame> tag.

Add the *<noframes>* tag for browsers that do not support frames.

You cannot use the *<body></body>* tags together with the *<frameset></frameset>* tags! See the next example.

How to use the <noframes> tag

There is no way to display a different content in browsers that don't support frames. Any browser that supports frames will see the frames- they wouldn't see anything inside <body> tag. Other browsers will see the message displayed inside <body> tag. The example is given in the code below:

<frameset cols="25%,50%,25%">
<frame src="frame_a.htm">
<frame src="frame_b.htm">
<frame src="frame_c.htm"><noframes>
<body>This browser cannot show frames!</body>
</noframes>
</frameset>

Mixed frameset

Now see how to make a frameset with three documents, and how to mix them in rows and columns.

<frameset rows="50%,50%">
<frame src="frame_a.htm">
<frameset cols="25%,75%">
<frame src="frame_b.htm">
<frame src="frame_c.htm">
</frameset>
</frameset>

Frameset with noresize

You may have noticed in our previous examples, the frames can be resized. Now we show you a simple way to make your frame non-resizable.

<frameset rows="50%,50%">
<frame noresize="noresize" src="frame_a.htm">
<frame noresize="noresize" src="frame_b.htm">
</frameset>

After viewing this code in your browser, move the mouse over the borders between the frames and notice that you cannot move the borders.

31

Frame navigation.

Save the three links below to a file named "links.htm". You must also create three files in the same folder for each link- frame_a.htm, frame_b.htm and frame_c.htm respectively.

*<a href ="frame_a.htm" target ="showframe">Frame a</a>
*
*<a href ="frame_b.htm" target ="showframe">Frame b</a>
*
<a href ="frame_c.htm" target ="showframe">Frame c</a>

Then create another page "index.htm" using the codes below. Ensure both links.htm and index.htm are saved to the same folder in the root of your testing server. The second frame will show the linked document.

<frameset cols="120,">*
<frame src="links.htm">
<frame src="frame_a.htm" name="showframe">
</frameset>

Open index.htm in your browser. The links are in your left. As you click, you see the frames navigate.

Inline frame

Iframe is used to create an inline frame (i.e. a frame inside an HTML page). Many developers use iframe to display Facebook "Like" buttons on their website.

<iframe src="demo_iframe.htm"></iframe>
<p>Old browsers don't support iframes.</p>
<p>If they don't, the iframe will not be visible.</p>

Jump to a specified section with frame navigation.

This example contain two frames. The navigation frame (main_content.htm) to the left contains a list of links with the second frame (links.htm) as a target. The second frame shows the linked document. One of the links in the navigation frame points to a specified section in the target file.

The HTML code in the file "main_content.htm" looks like this:

*<a href ="link.htm" target ="showframe">Link without Anchor</a>
*
<a href ="link.htm#C10" target ="showframe">Link with Anchor</a>.

The HTML code for link.htm:

<html><head></head><body>

```html
<a name="C1"><h2>Chapter 1</h2>
<p>This chapter explains ba bla bla</p>
</a><a name="C2"><h2>Chapter 2</h2>
<p>This chapter explains ba bla bla</p>
</a><a name="C3"><h2>Chapter 3</h2>
<p>This chapter explains ba bla bla</p>
</a><a name="C4"><h2>Chapter 4</h2>
<p>This chapter explains ba bla bla</p>
</a><a name="C5"><h2>Chapter 5</h2>
<p>This chapter explains ba bla bla</p>
</a><a name="C6"><h2>Chapter 6</h2>
<p>This chapter explains ba bla bla</p>
</a><a name="C7"><h2>Chapter 7</h2>
<p>This chapter explains ba bla bla</p>
</a><a name="C8"><h2>Chapter 8</h2>
<p>This chapter explains ba bla bla</p>
</a><a name="C9"><h2>Chapter 9</h2>
<p>This chapter explains ba bla bla</p>
</a><a name="C10"><h2>Chapter 10</h2></a>
<p>This chapter explains ba bla bla</p>
<a name="C11"><h2>Chapter 11</h2>
<p>This chapter explains ba bla bla</p>
</a><a name="C12"><h2>Chapter 12</h2>
<p>This chapter explains ba bla bla</p>
</a><a name="C13"><h2>Chapter 13</h2>
<p>This chapter explains ba bla bla</p>
</a><a name="C14"><h2>Chapter 14</h2>
<p>This chapter explains ba bla bla</p>
</a><a name="C15"><h2>Chapter 15</h2>
<p>This chapter explains ba bla bla</p>
</a><a name="C16"><h2>Chapter 16</h2>
<p>This chapter explains ba bla bla</p>
</a><a name="C17"><h2>Chapter 17</h2>
<p>This chapter explains ba bla bla</p>
</a></body></html>
```

The html code for index.htm:

```
<frameset cols="180,*">
<frame src="content.htm">
<frame src="link.htm" name="showframe">
</frameset>
```

12 HTML HEAD ELEMENT

The head element contains Meta elements, Page Title, Style and JavaScript. Only a few tags can be used inside the head section. They include: <base>, <link>, <meta>, <title>, <style> and <script> tags. The <link> tag goes there only when your style sheet is external.

Your HTML should be structured like this:
<html>
<head>
<title>My HTML Guide by Ohwofosirai Desmond</title>
<meta name="description" content="...Describe what your website contain here..."/>
<meta name="keyword" content="...a comma-separated list of keywords..."/>
<style>...CSS codes here...</style>
<script>...JavaScript codes here (if any)...</script>
</head>
<body>
....All other codes here...
</body>
<html>

So, this would be an illegal construct:
<head>
<p>My programming guide</p>
</head>
Here, the browser has two options: one, display the text because it is inside a paragraph; two, hide the text because it is in the wrong position.
All html elements except those ones permitted for use within the *<head>* segment, must go under the <body> segment. For example, *<p>*, *<em>*, *<h1>*, *<div>*, *<span>*, *<table>*, *<form>*, etc must be nested within the *<body>* tag.

13 STYLESHEETS

Like I said earlier, a style sheet beautifies your page, giving it a good look and feel, at the same time saving resources. When a browser reads a style sheet, it will format the document according to its specifications. There are three ways of inserting a style sheet:

External Style Sheet

An external style sheet is ideal when the style is applied to many pages. All formatting are moved out of the HTML document into a separate style sheet. With an external style sheet, you can change the look of an entire Web site by changing contents on one file. Each page must link to the style sheet using the <link> tag. The <link> tag goes inside the head section. The link anchor "href" points to the location of the sheet style. If it's somewhere on the internet, you begin with *http://*.

<head>
<link rel="stylesheet" type="text/css" href="mystyle.css">
</head>
Notice that in the head section *<style>* tag is replaced by *<link>*.

How do we create an external style sheet?
You simply open a blank page. Enter CSS codes without any *<style>* tag like this:
body{background-color: black; margin:5em;}
h1{text-align:center; color: white}
p{margin-top:6px;padding:0;}
#center{border:1px solid #aaa}

The code maybe as short as the one above, but notice there is no <style> tag anywhere. Save as "mystyle.css". You must save your CSS file name with ".css" file extension.

Internal Style Sheet

An internal style sheet should be used when a single document has a unique style. You define internal styles in the head section with the <style> tag.
<html>

36

```
<head>
<style type="text/css">
body {background-color: red}
p {margin-left: 20px; color: red}
</style>
</head>
<body>
Check the color difference
<p>Just my style</p>
</body>
</html>
```

We will use the internal style sheet in our examples shortly.

Inline Styles

An inline style should be used when a unique style is to be applied to a single or few elements.

To use inline styles you use the style attribute in the relevant tag. The style attribute can contain any CSS property. The example shows how to change the color and the left margin of a paragraph:

```
<p style="color: red; margin-left: 20px">
This is a paragraph
</p>
```

You can try it for any other element of your choice- it works for table, body, span, div, p, h1, just name it!

Example:

In the example below, you will learn what you need to know as a beginner. But don't forget to ask questions in case you need help. You can also check out our tutorial blog for more examples.

Style Sheet Tutorial

Enter your Email

[Subscribe]

Go Back

The Code Segment:

```
<html>
<title>How to use internal style sheet</title>
<style>
/* internal style sheet */
 body{color:black; font-family: verdana, arial}
 p{border:1px solid red; font-size:11px}
div a{text-decoration:none;}
input, button{height:3em; width:20em; padding:3px; margin:10px;margin-
left:40px}
div, #note{float:left; background-color:brown; color: white}
form{width:22em; clear:both; padding:5px}
/* internal style sheet ends */
</style>
<head>
<body>
<!- -inline CSS in h1 below- ->
<h1 style="color:#333">Style Sheet Tutorial</h1>
<span id="note">Enter your Email</span>
<form>
<p>
<input type="text" name="e-mail"/><br/>
<button type="button" id="button">Subscribe</button>
</p>
</form>
```

```
<div>
<a href="#">Go Back</a>
</div>
</body>
</html>
```

Explanation:

Looking at the internal style sheet, you notice html elements like body, h1, div, p, etc. Any property we assign to them would apply wherever the elements occur throughout the page. Every property of body element applies to the whole page. For example, if we have *"body{color:red}"*, the entire texts in the page will be red. In HTML properties can be inherited from bigger family. Such properties inherited from the bigger family can be overridden when a smaller section has its own property assigned to it. That's why even when we made the body text color black, there is still a white text.

You can also notice from the internal style sheet that "#" preceded "note", its because "note" is not a html element. If it were, you would see something like <note> within the body element". Rather, what you see is *id="note"*. Id is used as an attribute for html element "span". So if we have more than one "span" in your code, the id would help the browser know which one has the property being assigned. You may use "class" instead of id, the only difference is that in the internal style sheet (head section), you must then precede "note" with ".". Instead of "#". They are functionally the same.

You will also notice "div, #note" in the internal style sheet. All occurences of '<div>" and 'id="note"' within elements, will both possess the same properties specified within {}. Also you see "div a". In that case, the property specified within {} only applies to the (or those) <a> tag(s) that are found within a <div> tag.

By default, all links are blue and are underlined. The *"text decoration:none"* enable us remove the line. You can set to "underline", "blink" or "none". The spacing can be set using Padding-left, padding-right, padding-top-padding-bottom, margin-right, margin-left, margin-top or margin-bottom. The value is either in px or em. Font-family can be set to verdana, sans serif, trebuchet MS, arial, Helvetica, Harrington, etc.

EXERCISE

1)   Find out the difference between HTML elements "div" and "span".
2)   Partition your web page (full screen) to four equal parts (two columns, two rows) with "table" and with "div".

14 HTML META

The Meta Element

Meta means "Information About Something". We use html meta element to provide information about an html document.

More often, we use meta element to provide information that is important to browsers or search engines. For example, we supply keywords and describe the content of our document using the most relevant meta elements.

Meta Keyword & Description

Some search engines on the internet will index your page using information provided by this meta elements.

Meta element describing your page:
<meta name="description" content="Online Tutorials based on PHP , CSS, XML and MySQL" />

Meta element with major page's keywords.
<meta name="keywords" content="HTML tutorial, web design, php programming, JQuery" />

 Many webmasters have used meta tags for spamming, like repeating keywords to give pages a higher ranking. So, many search engines except yahoo have stopped using them entirely.

You can read more about search engines optimization from our blog: http://tag4free.blogspot.com.

Strange Meta Attributes

Sometimes you will see a strange meta attribute like this:
<meta name="content-type" content="utf-8" />
Then it means it is unique to the site- so it has no relevance to you.
Sometime, people use meta tags for redirecting visitors or refreshing their web pages too. You can find out more about that on the internet.

15 HTML SCRIPT

We have earlier emphasized that the script element should be nested in the head section of your html, but if found inside the body segment, it will work fine too. We add scripts to HTML pages to make them dynamic and interactive.

Script inside HTML

We begin developing our script with <script> tag. Scripting language must be specified too using the type attribute. See example below:

```
<html>
<body>
<script type="text/javascript">
alert("my first code!")
</script>
</body>
</html>
```

The script above will just alert:
My first code!

Note: To learn more about scripting in HTML, read our jQuery Programming Guide.

Handle older browsers

A browser that does not recognize the <script> tag at all, will display the contents of the tag. To prevent this from happening, use comment tag to hide the script.
An old browser (that does not recognize the <script> tag) will ignore the comment and it will not write the tag's content on the page, while a new browser will understand that the script should be executed.

Example

```
<body>
<script type="text/javascript">
<!--
alert("my first script!")
```

```
//-->
</script>
</body>
```

Noscript Tag

you can also use a *<noscript>* tag for browsers that recognize the <script> tag, but do not support the script it contain, so these browsers will show the text inside the <noscript> tag.

Example
```
<script type="text/javascript">
<!--
alert("my first script!")
//-->
</script>
<noscript>Your browser is too old!</noscript>
```

If you want to learn more about JavaScript, you should study our jQuery Programmer Guide.

16 TURN YOUR PC TO WEB SERVER

WAMP – Windows, Apache, MySQL and PHP

WAMP is a bundle of preconfigured applications which enable you use your local computer like an internet server for testing PHP codes. You can then see the demo of your scripts- how it will look when hosted on the internet.

It eliminates the stress of reconfiguring individual applications like MySQL, PHP and Apache after installation. Once installed, Server is ready. No further configuration needed.

WAMP comes with Apache Internet Server, MySQL Database, and PHP interpreter. All pre-configured to work together as a unit.

WAMP is free and open source. It can be readily downloaded from the internet any day.

After you have downloaded and installed WAMP Server follow these steps:

Look for a new folder called wamp on your hard drive i.e. C:\Wamp

Open the Wamp folder, and find a folder named www

Create a new folder, named "MyApp", under www.

Write some PHP or HTML code and save the file as "example.php" in the new folder

Make sure your Web server is running (see below)

Open your browser and type "http://localhost/MyApp/example.php" , to view your first web page

Note: Look for the WAMP symbol in your start menu or desktop. Click on it to start your server.

HTML COLORS

HTML Colors are displayed in combination of RED, GREEN, and BLUE light i.e. RGB. W3C listed 16 color names valid for HTML and CSS:
aqua, blue, black, fuchsia, green, gray, lime, maroon, olive, navy, purple, red, silver, white, teal and yellow.

In our example codes, you can try out the color given below:

Brown	#A52A2A	DeepPink	#FF1493
BurlyWood	#DEB887	DeepSkyBlue	#00BFFF
CadetBlue	#5F9EA0	DimGray	#696969
Chocolate	#D2691E	DodgerBlue	#1E90FF
Coral	#FF7F50	FireBrick	#B22222
CornflowerBlue	#6495ED	FloralWhite	#FFFAF0
Cornsilk	#FFF8DC	Gold	#FFD700
Crimson	#DC143C	GoldenRod	#DAA520
Cyan	#00FFFF	Gray	#808080
DarkBlue	#00008B	Green	#008000
DarkCyan	#008B8B	GreenYellow	#ADFF2F
DarkGray	#A9A9A9	HoneyDew	#F0FFF0
DarkGreen	#006400	HotPink	#FF69B4
DarkKhaki	#BDB76B	IndianRed	#CD5C5C
DarkMagenta	#8B008B	Indigo	#4B0082

LightBlue	#ADD8E6	SlateBlue	#6A5ACD
LightCoral	#F08080	SlateGray	#708090
LightYellow	#FFFFE0	Snow	#FFFAFA
Lime	#00FF00	SpringGreen	#00FF7F
LimeGreen	#32CD32	SteelBlue	#4682B4
Linen	#FAF0E6	Teal	#008080
Magenta	#FF00FF	Thistle	#D8BFD8
Maroon	#800000	Tomato	#FF6347
PowderBlue	#B0E0E6	Turquoise	#40E0D0
Purple	#800080	Violet	#EE82EE
Red	#FF0000	Wheat	#F5DEB3
Silver	#C0C0C0	White	#FFFFFF
SkyBlue	#87CEEB	WhiteSmoke	#F5F5F5

CONCLUSION

This tutorial has taught you how to use HTML to create your own web site.
So What's Next?
The next step is to learn PHP and JQUERY.

Jquery

If you are interested in web technology, you must learn jQuery. It's a very important component of many web2.0 sites (including Facebook) which make you impressed. Without it I bet Facebook wouldn't freak you.
If you want to learn more about JQUERY, read our JQUERY PROGRAMMER GUIDE.

PHP

PHP enables you to handle database. Without it (or any other scripting language) you cannot create forums, chatting sites, blogs, e-commerce sites or even your dream application. They all use databases.
To learn PHP, read our PHP PROGRAMMER GUIDE.

Have any questions? Feel free to contact me:
mailto:dexmundo@gmail.com,
Phone: +2347067064993
Blog: http://tag4free.blogspot.com
Facebook: www.facebook.com/dexmundo

www.ingramcontent.com/pod-product-compliance
Lightning Source LLC
Chambersburg PA
CBHW061044050326
40689CB00012B/2964